A SEASON
OF COMFORT

MAL AUSTIN

HOWARD BOOKS
A DIVISION OF SIMON & SCHUSTER
New York   London   Toronto   Sydney

picture · psalms   *an illustrated meditation*

INTRODUCTION

The tree has been a constant in the lives of humans and animals since the beginning of time.

Creative minds have forever recorded stories, whether true or imagined, with the friendly tree playing an integral part. Trees have offered shelter, protection, escape, fascination, inspiration and comfort for many in times of need. From a little girl lost in the forest to an adventurous boy to a group of desperate fugitives, all have appreciated the forest's welcoming shelter and found comfort in the canopy trees offer for shade or the branches they offer for escape.

Lumberjacks find comfort as they rely on the tree for income and support; the builder finds comfort as he hammers into sturdy wood to complete his project: the birds and animals find comfort as they seek protection and food in the trees.

One of the beautiful things about trees is that they come in all sizes and shapes and strengths and shortcomings. Like humans, they come from different families and types, sometimes even in two genders. Some trees seem small and insignificant, but bear great fruit, while others look grand and strong, but don't really offer much. All are affected in some way by the seasons; some produce vivid color as their endearing quality, while others offer strength and power.

While the Bible mentions flowers just under two hundred times, trees rate ten times the room.

Trees have long been a subject of discussion in the Bible, from practical building matters to a symbol of steadfastness and integrity. God truly created something beautiful in trees, and perhaps the best is yet to be. In I Chronicles 16:33 scripture tells us the "the trees will sing with joy," giving us a tiny glimpse of what might be in store for us after the Lord returns.

Reality dictates that most of the trees in the forests and the landscapes that I pass swiftly by in my car on a journey to a location are not likely to hold any great interest for me. Yet some trees provide my most treasured and revered subjects. I know where all these are; some of them are pictured in this book. I have often found these special little areas by accident, and they are the keepers of some of my most important photographic and mystical memories.

Photographically, trees provide the patterns, textures, lines, and shapes for which I search. As a believer in one Creator I am easily able to see His hand in their variety and uniqueness, to hear His voice in their rustle, and to use them, as I often have, as walls for a fortress when I seek an uninterrupted conversation with God.

They are my great friends; and some of them should know me well, as I return to them regularly and try to capture them in just a little better way than the last time I paid them a visit.

About the Photographer

Mal Austin is one of Australia's most prominent Christian artists with a camera. A former schoolteacher, Mal now devotes his time to capturing the beauty of nature and crafting it into posters, gift cards, calendars, and books.

Eighteen years of commercial photography saw him complete over 650 weddings and hundreds of family portraits and advertising assignments. In 2000, Mal began a new photographic direction and vision under the name of Givenworks, believing God had given him new works to do. He specializes in the use of a panoramic film camera, and his work takes him deep into the Australian and New Zealand countryside to capture many isolated places with untouched landscapes.

Mal also works in close-up floral images with an emphasis on color, pattern, shape, and texture. While some images used in this book are from large-format Pentax and Bronica film cameras, most are digitally captured using Nikon D70 and D80 cameras.

www.givenworks.com

VARIETY
Trees and trees and trees. All of life's differences, contrasts, and variety—even a few mysteries—seem to be summarized in the world's great collection of trees.

COLOR
Not just brown! Every kind of gray, ocher, green, red, and brown is on display. We're sure to find at least some colors we love!

LIGHT
The forest cannot live without light, and even though it seems to come and go in different strengths, it is a constant source of strength and beauty—because it was designed to be that way.

SIZE
Overwhelming, intimidating structures of strength and imposing presence; twisted, contorted, and half the size that good rain could produce; fragile youngsters desperate for establishment—all belong.

SOUND
Stillness and peace are found here. Then later the sounds of collision, rushing wind, rain; a varied symphony of life and change.

PATTERNS
From the most rigid man-made order of the pine plantation to the repetitive chaos of a scrubby forest, and the patterns on bark, everywhere in the forest, something can be seen over and over again.

SHAPE
Millions of leaves and trunks can own the same name and makeup, but all are unique. What massive creative source is able to achieve that?

COMMUNITY
At once both brothers and opponents; competing for resources, fighting for light and food, yet thrown together as a collective force of size and significance, belonging together.

INDEPENDENCE
I can help, improve, add, subtract, and destroy, but if I leave a tree entirely alone, it will not need anything from me!

Psalm 103

Comfort in God's Love

His name is Holy

PRAISE THE LORD, O MY SOUL;
ALL MY INMOST BEING,
PRAISE HIS HOLY NAME.

PRAISE THE LORD, O MY SOUL,

AND FORGET NOT ALL HIS BENEFITS—

Praise the Lord

WHO FORGIVES ALL YOUR SINS
AND HEALS ALL YOUR DISEASES,
WHO REDEEMS YOUR LIFE
FROM THE PIT
AND CROWNS YOU
WITH LOVE AND
COMPASSION,
WHO SATISFIES YOUR DESIRES
WITH GOOD THINGS
SO THAT YOUR YOUTH
IS RENEWED
LIKE THE EAGLE'S.

the Lord works righteousness and justice
for all the oppressed

righteousness

he made known his ways to Moses,
his deeds to the people of Israel

justice

THE LORD IS
COMPASSIONATE
AND GRACIOUS,

gracious

SLOW TO ANGER,
ABOUNDING
IN LOVE.

He will not always accuse,
nor will he harbor
his anger forever;
he does not treat us
as our sins deserve
or repay us
according to our iniquities.

so great is his love

FOR AS HIGH AS THE HEAVENS ARE ABOVE THE EARTH,
SO GREAT IS HIS LOVE FOR THOSE WHO FEAR HIM;
AS FAR AS THE EAST IS FROM THE WEST,
SO FAR HAS HE REMOVED OUR TRANSGRESSIONS FROM US.

As a father has compassion
on his children,
so the Lord has compassion
on those who fear him;
for he knows how
we are formed,
he remembers
that we are dust.

fear him

AS FOR MAN, HIS DAYS ARE LIKE GRASS,
HE FLOURISHES LIKE A FLOWER OF THE FIELD;

THE WIND BLOWS OVER IT AND IT IS GONE,

AND ITS PLACE REMEMBERS IT NO MORE.

flower of the field

keep his covenant

BUT FROM EVERLASTING TO EVERLASTING
THE LORD'S LOVE IS WITH THOSE WHO FEAR HIM,

ND HIS RIGHTEOUSNESS WITH THEIR CHILDREN'S CHILDREN—
WITH THOSE WHO KEEP HIS COVENANT
AND REMEMBER TO OBEY HIS PRECEPTS.

The Lord has
established His throne
in heaven,
and his kingdom
rules over all.

rules over all

PRAISE THE LORD, YOU HIS ANGELS,

YOU MIGHTY ONES WHO DO HIS BIDDING,

WHO OBEY HIS WORD.

PRAISE THE LORD, ALL HIS HEAVENLY HOSTS,
YOU HIS SERVANTS WHO DO HIS WILL.

praise the Lord, O my soul

PRAISE THE LORD, ALL HIS WORKS

EVERYWHERE IN HIS DOMINION.

PRAISE THE LORD, O MY SOUL.

PSALM 112

Comfort Through Faith in God

PRAISE THE LORD!

BLESSED IS THE MAN WHO FEARS THE LORD,

WHO FINDS GREAT DELIGHT IN HIS COMMANDS.

HIS CHILDREN WILL BE MIGHTY IN THE LAND;
THE GENERATION OF THE UPRIGHT WILL BE BLESSED.

be blessed

WEALTH AND RICHES
ARE IN HIS HOUSE,
AND HIS
RIGHTEOUSNESS
ENDURES FOREVER.

His love endures forever

gracious and compas

EVEN IN DARKNESS LIGHT DAWNS FOR THE UPRIGHT,

FOR THE GRACIOUS AND COMPASSIONATE

AND RIGHTEOUS MAN.

GOOD WILL COME TO HIM WHO IS

GENEROUS AND LENDS FREELY,

WHO CONDUCTS HIS AFFAIRS WITH JUSTICE.

SURELY HE WILL NEVER BE SHAKEN;

a righteous man

A RIGHTEOUS MAN WILL BE REMEMBERED FOREVER.

HE WILL HAVE NO FEAR OF BAD NEWS;

triumph on his foes

HIS HEART IS STEADFAST, TRUSTING IN THE LORD.

HIS HEART IS SECURE, HE WILL HAVE NO FEAR;

IN THE END HE WILL LOOK IN TRIUMPH ON HIS FOES.